SCULPTURE IN WOOD

1.   P. EDWARD NORMAN.   *The Osteopath*, wood, with pelvis and spine in ivory

SCULPTURE IN WOOD

P. EDWARD NORMAN

A.R.C.A., A.T.D.

LONDON / **ALEC TIRANTI** / 1969

1st edition (Studio Books) 1954
Present revised edition 1962, 1969

PRINTED BY THE DEVONSHIRE PRESS, TORQUAY

BOUND BY C. & H. T. EVANS, CROYDON

© ALEC TIRANTI LTD., 72 CHARLOTTE STREET, LONDON, W.1

MADE AND PRINTED IN THE UNITED KINGDOM

(GB) SBN 85458 958/9

CONTENTS

ACKNOWLEDGMENTS

Grateful acknowledgment is made to Alan Durst, A.R.A., under whom I studied at the Royal College of Art, and to his book *Wood Carving*, first published by The Studio Ltd. in 1938; to E. Owen Jennings, Esq., Principal of Tunbridge Wells School of Art; to the sculptors and students who have kindly lent their work for reproduction; to R. E. Gower, Esq., who is responsible for many of the photographs; and to others who have assisted in producing this book.

FOREWORD

As far back in the history of the world as man is known to have existed he has fashioned objects in a variety of materials, stones, flints, bone, wood and ivory; because of its perishable nature early articles in wood are rare, but being easier to work compared with the other materials wood must have been very evident and much used.

The beasts he hunted and killed were often subjects for his expression; a terrifying experience, a nearness to death may have prompted him to portray in wood or stone the animal, or characteristics of the animal, which he encountered. This carving or sculpture, albeit very crude, is sufficient in itself to show this inborn desire in man to express himself through the visual art of sculpture.

The early carvings and scratchings which have been found show a wonderful spontaneity, they are truly free and uninfluenced by any other work. They show man happy in his ability to create, however crudely, a vision, expression or experience through form.

So it has been all through the ages; the fragments of sculpture, pieces of wood fashioned to beautiful shapes or exquisitely carved to tell a story, such as the Gothic enrichments which have come down to us, serve as a guide to Man, his environment, mode of life, and the personalities and things he was acquainted with during his lifetime.

Man's technical skill, both in the design and construction of his tools, and his ability to use them, grew; he found new methods, new approaches, his field of accomplishment broadened and finally became so great that the artistic expression of his innermost being was almost lost in the skill of his hands.

To the layman who, on rare occasions, sees these carvings during one of his all too infrequent visits to a museum of art treasures, the realization that these carvings have been wrought by hand, by the humble artist-crafts man, is not always very acute; he is probably so concerned with the technique and subject matter contained therein that any thought of being able to carve something himself in wood does not even enter his mind.

If this man could be conducted through the museum's treasures starting at the simplest objects and have explained to him, their meaning and the technique involved in their execution, he might feel a desire to attempt a simple piece of carving himself: he would not feel afraid of criticism through trying to carve something which at first sight appears simple and childish; and having carved something which he is able to complete and master he will feel the desire to go on and attempt something a little more ambitious: he will want to see more examples of work, study them and see how certain passages have been accomplished, how the material has been considered, used to its best advantage, and perhaps how an idea or theme has been treated by sculpture of various periods.

When this desire to create has been awakened, and with a few tools to hand, then is the time for him to carve. Mistakes will be made, there will be many, wood will be found to be extremely unco-operative in his early efforts: but these difficulties, if he is keen, will serve only to goad him on to surmount and to conquer them.

In this book, I have in mind not the skilled and accomplished sculptor, but the young student beginning to carve, or the person who has some interest in the subject of sculpture but feels he needs some early guidance. I have used several illustrations of wood sculpture done by young students, none of whom I would say has carved for a period exceeding two years. The carvings are fairly small and suitable for indoor decoration, they are compact and pleasant to feel and touch, and of a size which will not prohibit their being done 'at home'.

Some of the carvings are simple, some perhaps a little crude, but they have all been included to illustrate a particular point.

The way the material is carved, although very necessary to know and understand, is not all-important. Rather should the design, the expression and the aesthetic quality of the work be of primary importance. The skill of manipulating the tools, and knowing which to use, will come with practice and experience. The design will come, first with guidance, and secondly by seeing work as frequently as possible. While looking at work try to realise its subtler and deeper meaning and think back from the finished work through its various stages to the original piece of material.

The student should at all times create, and not become a slave to copy work: he must be willing to experiment, to accept new methods, fresh materials and fresh ideas: and by so doing his work will retain that liveliness and spirit and freedom which is so essential to wood sculpture.

TOOLS AND EQUIPMENT

As in all handicrafts the art of wood carving is one which necessitates the use of a number of tools of varying size and section. The number and variety of these will necessarily differ with the individual, the type and character of work to be executed and the craftsman's making or adapting tools to suit his needs for a particular piece of carving. But carving can be achieved with the use of very few and sometimes even primitive tools: simple knives, scrapers, even sharpened nails (as witness the carvings produced by prisoners of war), but naturally with more elementary tools, the skill, perseverance and ingenuity of the carver will need to be of a high level.

Consider the wooden knife, fork and spoon shown in figure 2. 'Here is a delicacy and sureness of touch to delight the connoisseur of wood carvings. The traditional Chinese dragon crouches identically in each piece, dynamic in treatment, awaiting only the passing of a magic wand to unleash itself. Every detail is present and one must count the individual tool marks to discover any dissimilarity in the trio.

'But these carvings are not the work of some aged Chinese craftsman. Incredible though it may seem, they were fashioned by a nine-year-old Chinese boy, produced with "tools" at which the Western craftsman would stand aghast. A knife ground from a broken file, a gouge made from an old nail, pieces of glass and bits of iron from the scrap-heap—such were the tools and such are still used to-day in the ramshackle workshops which abound in the old City of Shanghai.'[1]

To commence with perhaps five or six gouges and chisels will be sufficient, together with a wood rasp of half-round section, one or two rifflers, a wood mallet, a sharpening stone and gouge slip, lubricating oil, or neats foot oil, a saw, a tenon saw. Then we shall want a strong bench of comfortable height about 38 to 40 inches from ground to bench level, and this should be placed in the workshop where a good strong natural light falls on it. It should also be placed so that movement is impossible, and the use of metal brackets securing the legs of the bench to the ground is advisable, as the force necessary to remove wood at the early stages of a

[1] *Wood Carvings of Peasant China* by W. A. G. Bradman: *The Studio.*

3

2. *Knife, fork and spoon, the work of a nine-year-old Chinese boy*

carving is considerable and quite sufficient to gradually work a bench along the floor.

Next will come the problem of holding wood securely whilst it is being carved, and this may be done by placing the work in a vice which is capable of being opened at least 10 inches. The jaws of this vice must be provided with cork and buff pieces to prevent injury to the carving and to the tools being used.

A couple of good stout G clamps are also extremely useful for holding the work to the bench top, as they permit the work to be seen more easily and also moved about freely for the various directions of cut which will be necessary. Another method of holding work quite firmly is to screw it to another piece of close-grained wood of about $1\frac{1}{2}$ inch thickness with 4 inch wood screws and then to clamp this piece of wood to the edge of the bench.

The main point is that the work should be at a comfortable height and distance that one does not have to bend downwards or backwards unduly, that it can be moved easily to be able to work on different parts, and that it is placed in good light so that every cut made is easily visible.

Other items to have handy are a piece of chalk, crayon or charcoal for marking or sketching on the work, and a first aid outfit in case of small accidents either when handling or sharpening the tools, or during the actual carving process.

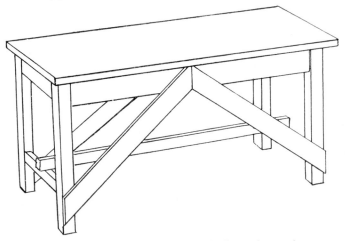

3. *Bench constructed of wood with diagonal cross braces for extra strength*

The gouge. This tool is usually recognised by the width and curvature of its blade or cutting edge—the curve is called the sweep, and may vary from a deep U section to almost flat. The most popular widths are from $\frac{1}{8}$ inch to 1 inch. The blade is ground on the outside edge, the inside remains straight, at least for all our purposes. The angle of this bevel will vary slightly depending on the size of the tool, being somewhat longer in the large sweep and becoming shorter in the smaller and more delicate tools. Since the larger gouges are used for the preliminary work of setting, or 'bosting' out the work and are subject to heavy blows with the mallet, the reason for keeping the bevel short and rather stout will be obvious.

The flatter and smaller gouges are used for finishing and for more intricate details, and since very often they are used with hand pressure only, the bevel may be long, and the sharpness of the tool must be maintained at all times.

5

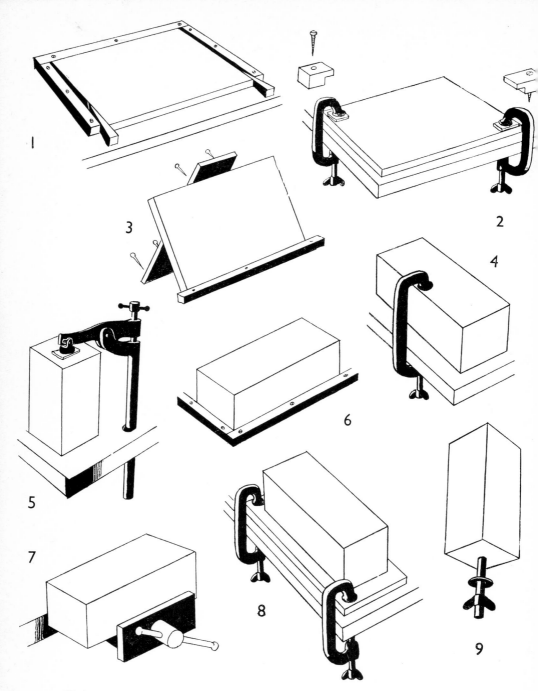

4. *Various ways of holding the wood: 1-3 are for holding flat panels; 4-9 for holding blocks of wood. All these methods allow quick and easy moving of the wood when necessary*

Carvers in the past have used a great range of gouges, i.e. veiners, spoon bends, salmon bends, back bends, macaroni, spade form and a host of others, all these shapes and variations indeed being necessary when such objects as bunches of grapes and fruit, reproductions of antique furniture and wall decorations, etc., work with intricate undercutting and difficult passages to execute cleanly, were being carved. But this type of work is not covered here and all these implements seem hardly necessary for us to include in our tool kit.

The chisels. It is as well to have chisels of about $\frac{1}{2}$ inch and 1 inch blade for straight edges and these should be ground both sides to have a symmetrical cutting edge. Another chisel of about $\frac{3}{8}$ inch blade width, with the blade ground to an angle of about $40°$ (corner chisel), will be useful for cutting into corners and for lining-in work in relief.

Very small gouges or chisels, rather more like engravers', may be made by obtaining a length of $\frac{1}{8}$ inch diameter silver steel rod, cutting it into 4-inch lengths, the end of each piece then being suitably shaped by means of a file and grindstone. This end should next be hardened by heating about an inch to red, and plunging it in cold water (this will make the steel hard but brittle). The end should be cleaned off with a piece of emery cloth. Now gently heat the metal again, ensuring that the small flame plays about an inch from the cutting end. Watch the colour of the metal: it will appear to turn a blueish shade, which will travel toward the tip. Immediately this is reached plunge the metal in water. The cutting edge will now be suitable for cutting most woods including lignum vitae.

Handles may be fashioned by cutting off lengths from $\frac{1}{2}$ or $\frac{3}{4}$ inch wood dowel, drilling the end, and inserting the end of the silver steel rod. The cutting edge may then be sharpened on a sharpening stone and slip.

It is advisable to keep the ends of these small home-made tools covered with a cork to avoid damage. They are invaluable in small detail work, and I have used them with great success in ivory carving.

The tools should be kept in a baize cloth arranged in compartments to avoid the cutting edges coming into contact with each other. They should be rubbed occasionally with a slightly oily rag to prevent rust.

Sharpening stones. These are very essential parts of the carver's equipment and comprise:

> A Washita oilstone.
> An India slip.
> Various smaller slips (for the inside of gouges).
> A tin of lubricating oil (cycle oil is quite suitable).

5. *A selection of tools for carving. They include an oil can, gouge slip and oilstone, gouges of various widths and sweeps, a triangular scraper, a circular wood mallet, rifflers and a wood rasp. Should a tool become chipped or broken, it is advisable to take it to a local carpenter or tool merchant who will no doubt regrind it, often at the same time giving a practical demonstration of how to do this somewhat difficult task, for a very nominal charge*

To prevent it slipping the oilstone should be held at the corner of the bench by means of thin strips of wood tacked round it. This will allow the stone to be turned over easily, to enable both sides of the stone to be used and so prolong its useful life.

The other slips should be kept either in a tin or trough fitted to the side of the bench, thus helping to prevent unnecessary wood dust shavings, etc., getting on them. It is also useful to obtain a leather strop for honing the tools as this enables a really razor-like edge to be maintained.

FIGURE 6. WOODCARVING TOOLS AND EQUIPMENT

No. 1.   Straight chisel

No. 2.   Corner chisel

Nos. 3-9.   Straight gouges
No. 10.   Straight fluter
No. 11.   Straight veiner

No. 39.   Straight parting ('V') too
No. 41.   Ditto, closer cut

No. 21.   Bent grounders (up to $\frac{3}{16}$")
Bent chisels above that
Nos. 22-23.   Corner bent chisels, left and right hand

Nos. 24-30.   Bent gouges
No. 31.   Bent fluter
No. 32.   Bent veiner

Nos. 33-38.   Back-bent gouges

No. 43.   Bent parting tool
No. 44.   Ditto with closer cut

Spade tool: this short pod shank is highly useful for light work and can be had up to $\frac{3}{8}$"

Fishtails: very useful in 1" and over in place of the straight shanked tools which are clumsy in these bigger sizes

Octagonal handles give perfect grip and do not allow the tool to roll off the bench.   There are various sizes

9

STRAIGHT	BENT	BACKBENT (UP TO ½")	$\frac{1''}{32}$ 1mm	$\frac{1''}{16}$ 2mm	$\frac{1''}{8}$ 3mm	$\frac{5''}{32}$ 4mm	$\frac{3''}{16}$ 5mm	$\frac{1''}{4}$ 6½mm	$\frac{5''}{16}$ 8mm	$\frac{3''}{8}$ 9½mm	$\frac{7''}{16}$ 11mm
No. 1	No. 21	No.									
2	22·3										
3	24	33									
4	25	34									
5	26	35									
6	27	36									
7	28	37									
8	29	38									
9	30										
10	31										
11	32										
39	43										
41	44										

Each and every cut has its use. But for the beginners a simple set of the following six straight tools should be sufficient:

No. 1—$\frac{1}{2}$"   No. 5—$\frac{3}{4}$"
No. 3—$\frac{5}{8}$" (spade)   No. 6—$\frac{1}{2}$"
No. 4—$\frac{3}{8}$"   No. 9—$\frac{1}{4}$"

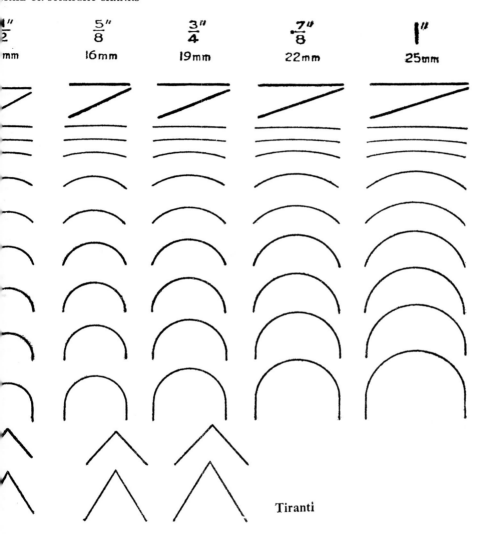

$\frac{1}{2}''$ $\frac{5''}{8}$ $\frac{3''}{4}$ $\frac{7''}{8}$ $1''$

mm   16mm   19mm   22mm   25mm

Tiranti

increase the set to twelve tools, add:

No. 2—$\frac{3}{8}''$ (corner or skew chisel)   No. 21—$\frac{3}{16}''$ (grounder)
No. 9—$\frac{1}{2}''$ No. 30—$\frac{1}{4}''$
No. 11—$\frac{1}{8}''$ (veiner)   No. 39—$\frac{1}{4}''$ (straight parting tool)

s set of twelve will vary according to teacher, school, special requirements, etc., but each
and every tool listed is a useful basic one

8. *Stones and slips. The stones are plain rectangular pieces and are for general sharpening. The slips are smaller, shaped, pieces for taking off burr on the inside of the tool*

9. *The bench screw is for holding a block of wood down firmly onto the bench. It goes through a hole in the bench with the wing screw underneath to tighten up*

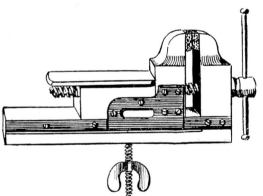

10. *The carver's chops, or wood vice, the essential maid-of-all-work for holding small figures and work in general. The jaws have cork and buff pieces so that the work is not bruised. The chops are fixed to the bench by a heavy screw which goes through a hole in the bench, and runs along the inside of the chops so that it can be pushed where required, and then fixed by tightening the wing nut*

11. *Hand-made rasp for quick yet smooth cutting*

WOODS

Woods, many types in number, vary from the soft and light balsa wood which may be cut with a sharp knife or razor blade, to the exceedingly hard African ironwoods and lignum vitae, requiring strong sharp gouges and a great deal of physical effort. Between these two extremes we have obeche, pine, elm, lime, sycamore, birch, holly, pear, plane, walnut, oak, mahogany, teak, jarrah, padauk, rosewood, ebony, snakewood, and many others all having their own peculiarities and suitability for individual pieces of carving.

It is as well when commencing to carve to choose a wood which is neither too hard nor soft and in which the grain is even, but not too pronounced. It should be as free as possible from knots, it should not have 'shakes' or cracks in its surface, and above all it should be perfectly seasoned and dry.

Now this question of seasoning is best left to the foreman of the timber merchant from whom the wood is purchased for he will know how long a particular piece has lain cut. Until one has acquired one's own stock of wood, stacked it suitably and then left it for a known number of years, it is best to rely on the timber man's advice and knowledge. Some of the harder woods mentioned at the end of the chapter are very difficult to procure, but occasionally it is possible to discover them in out-of-the-way country timber yards or in some of the London dock area warehouses. Small pieces of lignum vitae in the shape of bowls, balls and polo mallet heads may sometimes be obtained from junk shops or second-hand dealers.

A very important point to be considered is the grain of wood, because this greatly influences the cutting direction of the tool.

Take a block of, say, pine, and sand-paper smooth its ends and faces. Now examine the end and you will find what appears to be lines, forming segments of a circle, running across the wood. These lines are the annular lines of the wood and represent the growth of the tree; more important to us, they show that the grain is running from end to end along that block of wood.

It we were to take an axe, the wood could easily be split down its length, but it would be more difficult to cut across the block, because we should be chopping across the fibres of the wood. When we are going to commence a carving we must know in which direction the grain is running in relation to the block, so that our initial gouge cuts are made in the right direction.

Imagine for a moment that the block of wood is now a block of separate sheets of paper filed neatly on each other and that we are going to attempt to cut a corner off this pile with a sharp knife. If we attempt to cut from the end of the block or file at an angle towards the top, the knife will immediately pass between some of the sheets and continue in this direction against resistance to redirect it.

Now if we commence with the knife at the top of the block or file and cut slantwise towards the side, we shall be able to do so by cutting through the various layers which will come off one at a time until the cut is complete. This is exactly what happens when cutting the block of wood with gouge or chisel. If we drive the tool in the direction of the grain, the tool will be driven between the layers or fibres of the wood and split it. If the gouge is driven across the grain at an angle the wood will curl away, and we shall have removed the wood where, and in the direction, we wanted.

In some woods this grain problem is more acute because the wood itself is curly and in others more open or wavy (sycamore, etc.), and in some harder woods it is very difficult to see the grain at all: it is only with constant practice and an increasing knowledge of woods that these problems of direction of cut, etc., may be solved. It is a fairly safe rule to avoid cutting in exactly the same direction as the grain of the wood but always across it at an angle.

I have gone into the problem of the grain at some length because it is always present and I think is one of the main stumbling blocks to the person commencing carving in wood; but, with a little practice and experience, the problems are not so formidable as they may sound.

The shape of the block of wood is quite important, too, to the carver. Very often a piece of wood in its natural state will suggest a shape for carving, or its form may be developed and abstracted from its natural curves and twists. It is a good plan to have interesting shaped pieces of wood standing about in the studio or workshop, for quite often when one is in a contemplative mood inspiration is drawn from these shapes. Wood which has been cut to planks and rectangular form is not nearly so interesting, as the problem of transforming flat block forms into shapes which have movement and subtleties of planes is much more difficult.

Again, choice of wood which has interesting grain or figuring, or unusual markings, may help the movement, or feeling of growth or rhythm, which we need to portray. The colour of wood is also important as the amount of modelling a form requires is influenced by the light and its reflection,

12. A. S. GARBUTT. *Torso*, height about 24 inches. Notice the broad treatment of the main forms, and the way the grain of the wood emphasizes and enriches the modelling

and we normally find that a light wood will need a rather simpler treatment than a dark one.

The direction of the grain which is chosen for the work is important. Wood across a short grain is very prone to damage; for instance if we were carving a horse in wood, it would be advisable to have the grain running vertically, or in the main direction of the legs and tail, thus giving these somewhat thin parts rather more strength. In larger scale work it may become necessary to join the wood in various directions of the grain to obtain the required strength, and this applies rather more to work which is to be placed out of doors, larger figures, animals, symbols which are intended for inn signs, town emblems, heraldic devices, bearers, etc.

The illustration in figures 13-17 show the varied grain and figure in different woods. Figure 13. Walnut

14. Bird's eye maple

15. Indian rosewood

16. *Sycamore*

17. *Sycamore with less pronounced figure*

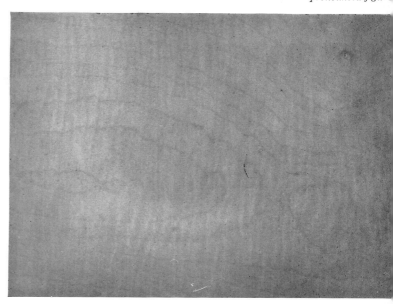

BIRCH: a good wood to carve in, has interesting flecks in its surfaces, pleasant light brown colour.

BOXWOOD: a hard yellow wood, very little grain evident; excellent for detail: sharp tools required; not obtainable in very large section.

CHERRY: excellent wood for carving; interesting even-textured grain.

EBONY: jet black wood; hard; good to carve with sharp tools; excellent finish.

ELM: has a twisted grain, which can be used to advantage for its decorative value, but wood is inclined to be stringy to carve; liable to warp.

HICKORY: white, even grain.

HOLLY: very white wood; hard; close.

JARRAH: a hard red colour; even grain.

KARRI: similar to jarrah, but harder, slightly coarser grain.

LAUREL: greenish brown colour; excellent to carve; beautiful polish.

LIGNUM VITAE: extremely hard; beautiful rich green brown colour; oily nature: a fine wood to carve; high polish.

LIME: a soft wood, light yellow in colour; rather uninteresting grain and texture; easy to carve.

MAHOGANY: beautiful colour varying from deep gold to rich red; hard.

OAK: a wood which has been used through the centuries by the carver. Strong, lovely grain and rich colour: requires broad treatment.

OBECHE: a light even grain yellow colour; not too easy to carve as it is soft and requires exceedingly sharp tools.

PADAUK: rich red colour, even grain.

PEAR: an excellent wood, cheesy in character to cut; very little grain; detail work may be accomplished; excellent finish.

PINE: requires very sharp tools and broad treatment; is fairly soft with hard grain fibres.

PLANE: similar to birch, but has very pronounced flecked figure.

ROSEWOOD: hard; rich purple brown colour; lovely finish.

SYCAMORE: a white wood rather more tricky to carve due to its somewhat curly grain. Will take an excellent finish.

TEAK: a strong grey wood, which seems slightly oily; cuts clearly and will give a beautiful finish; has deep brown colour. It is good for weathering out of doors. Tools will require sharpening often.

WALNUT (American and English): a beautiful wood to carve; cheesy in quality; deep rich brown colour—takes beautiful polish.

SHARPENING AND HOLDING
THE TOOLS

Now that we have our tools, sharpening stones and oil-can, it is necessary to learn how to sharpen the cutting edges. Good work can only be accomplished with sharp tools. Blunt or dull edges lead to torn wood and exasperation.

It will be best to start with a flat chisel of about 1-inch blade. As previously mentioned, this is usually ground to an equal bevel on both sides of the blade.

Drop a little oil on to the oilstone and stand with the stone in front of and in line with your body (the stone being held in position on the bench with the strips of wood). Lay the blade of the tool on the stone at about 15° angle, with the handle in the right hand, and two fingers of the left pressed on the blade near to the stone. The tool must then be rubbed from end to end of the stone, firmly and evenly, all the time at the same angle: this is most important, to ensure the same cutting angle is maintained. Exert pressure with the two fingers to maintain even contact with the stone. Practice the action carefully and slowly, and inspect the bevel occasionally to see that the correct angle and flatness is being maintained. When you are satisfied that this is so, and that the rubbing action has rubbed the steel bright as far as the cutting edge, turn the tool over and repeat the action for the other side.

When a keen edge is obtained, which can be tested by gently applying the finger, it should be stropped on the leather strop which has had a little emery paste applied to its surface. Strop both sides evenly to ensure that no burr is left on the cutting edge. If done correctly, it should now be ready for use, and may be tested across the grain of a piece of scrap wood.

The other flat chisels may be sharpened in the same way, but remember that the narrower the blade, the more exacting the sharpening process becomes.

When you are satisfied that the process of sharpening the flat chisels is satisfactory, you can pass on to a curved gouge.

Choose, a wide, flattish one. Commence rubbing up and down the stone as for the chisel, but in addition there is rotational movement. The gouge

18. Holding the tool for sharpening: the tool is held at the correct angle and moved from side to side with a slight rotation movement of the right wrist. The fingers of the left hand maintain a constant pressure on the blade. The slip is used to rub lightly inside the curve to remove any burr

must be rolled from side to side to bring all of the edge in turn in contact with the stone. Practice is needed to produce the correct wrist action, so that the rolling and up and down motion are in step with each other, and this is necessary to prevent the edge from receiving uneven attention which would result in a wavy edge. When you are satisfied that the outside edge is correct take the Indian slip and, finding the curve on the slip to correspond to the curve of the gouge, gently rub the tool along the slip to remove the burr but not to change the angle on the inside. Strop the tool on the leather, stropping the outside curve, and test the tool's edge for cutting keenness. Remove all traces of oil with a rag before touching the wood.

Another method of sharpening the gouge is to hold the tool in the right hand, with the blade resting on the oilstone, adjusting it to the correct angle; now commence to move the tool from one end of the stone to the other, at the same time rotating the wrist, so that all of the edge comes into contact with the stone at each stroke. Care must be taken to move the right hand parallel to the stone, and not let the tool form an arc. When the outside curve has been attended to in this way, the inside may be touched up with the gouge slip, as previously described.

Gouges with a deeper sweep and narrow blades must be sharpened in the same way, only remember more attention and care will be necessary.

Sharpening is a matter of concentrated practice.

The bevel should be a little shorter for extremely hard woods, and possibly for the large gouges used for setting or 'bosting' out.

Maintain the cutting edges in good condition, and occasionally wipe the blade with a slightly oily rag.

A good scheme is to mark the section of the cutting edge, near the top of the handle, so that you know the shape of the blade without removing the tool from its baize cover. This is particularly so when your tools have reached a considerable number.

When you are ready to commence carving you should lay out the few which you will need to begin with so that the cutting edge is easily visible.

Have a first aid box handy too, just in case you do have the misfortune to cut your finger.

Make sure that there is no oil on the bench or where it will get on to the wood. Once oil is there it is extremely difficult to remove, and it will soon soak in and discolour the wood.

Holding the tools. The gouge or chisel is held in the left hand, preferably with the thumb along the handle—this gives more control against the

19. *Using the mallet in the earlier and heavier stages of the work*

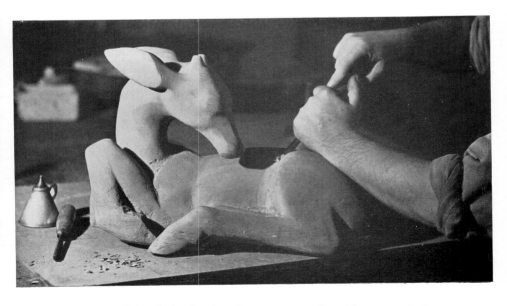

20. *Using the hands only, when more care and precision are required*

rotational movement of the tool which sometimes tends to occur, particularly when cutting in a curved surface.

The angle of the blade is a little more than the cutting bevel on the blade.

The gouge is driven by blows from the mallet. If the gouge has been driven too deeply into the wood do not attempt to remove it by rocking the tool about, as this may lead to a cracked or chipped edge. Take another gouge and lightly cut away wood around the tool until it can be freed. In some passages, and particularly in finishing stages, the mallet may be dispensed with and the tool held with the right hand over the end of the handle: the left hand grasping the upper end of the blade, and with a slight tendency to push against the right hand, controls it: in others just a gentle tapping of the tool with the hollow of the right hand will be sufficient. These two methods of holding the tools will come naturally with practice and as the problems of the work arise.

CARVING A FISH

CARVING A FISH . 1

I have described the tools, their sharpening and the equipment and wood necessary to carving. The next point is the choice of a subject. For a first exercise, I would suggest something which is fairly symmetrical and in which there is little or no movement.

I have chosen a simple but decorative fish shape. The first step is to get good references for our subject, either from book illustrations or photographs, and study them thoroughly, so as to become fully acquainted with the form we intend to make, its character and decorative value being of importance at this stage.

Good as photographs or drawings are, it is rather difficult to visualise the subject in three dimensions, that is length, depth and breadth, and I think it is as well to model our subject in clay, Plasticine or wax, not necessarily to a very high standard, and without much detail, to give something with thickness and substance from which rough dimensions (proportional) may be taken to obtain a likely piece of wood for the subject.

The silhouette shape would now be drawn on the wood with charcoal, chalk or crayon, and this outline shape cut out approximately with a saw. Do not attempt to cut round the curved lines. The more accurate outline shape is fashioned with either a wood rasp or a flat chisel. Remember, too, this outline is only an approximate guide and will be subject to adjustment as the work proceeds, and the design requires refinement. The wood is held during this preliminary process in a wood vice, which has cork and buff pieces between the jaws to prevent any undue bruising of the carving. Plate 21 shows the outline of the fish drawn on the wood, and then this shape simplified and reduced to straight lines for saw cutting, and the shape cut out. We are now ready to begin the carving of the form of the fish.

1. This shows the clay sketch, the reference and the block of wood with the outlines of the fish marked on and the main pieces removed from the block. The saw is the tool used in this stage

27

On the side of the fish indicate the true shape of the body as apart from the fins and tail; repeat this on the other side of the carving. Since it is symmetrical on both sides, draw a centre line round the edges of the wood: this will indicate the centre line of the fins and tail. The roughed-out shape may now be clamped down to the bench. Now take one of the broad gouges and, working from the indicated line of the body towards the edge of the fins, begin to remove the wood, taking care not to cut in at too steep an angle near the body, but rather making a gradual diminishing of the wood. Leave about $\frac{1}{4}$ inch from the centre line, to allow later finishing.

Remove the wood at the tail in the same way, and also the fins on the lower side. Turn the fish over and clamp down again, and repeat the same process, watching carefully to see that the fins, tail, etc., are not becoming too thin. It is as well to wedge odd scraps of wood under the fins, etc., to support them when they are being carved on the second side to help prevent any cracking while they are being thinned down.

Unclamp the work again and inspect it to see that the fins and tail appear quite central on the body, as indicated by the centre line you have drawn. If all is well we may proceed to the next stage.

We find that the eyes and the two small fins on each side of the body just behind the gills project a little from the main body of the fish. These should be drawn carefully in position on both sides of the fish.

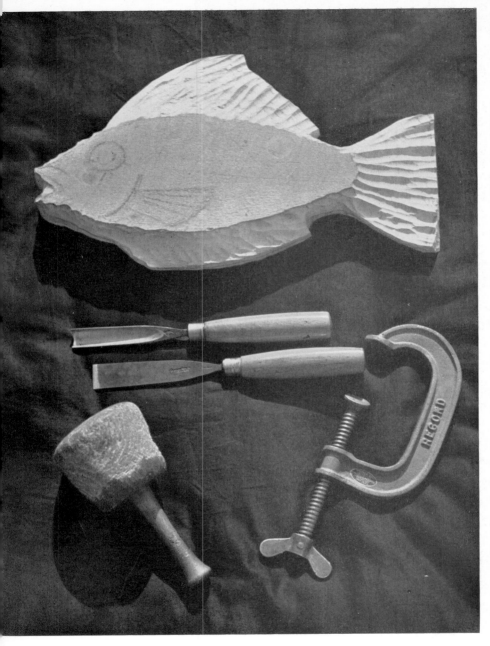

22. *The outline a little more carefully shaped. The carving of the fins and tail has been commenced. The deep and flattish gouges and the mallet are the tools used*

29

Clamp the work down again, and with one of the $\frac{1}{4}$-inch gouges and a rather flat sweep lightly cut down almost vertically round the outline of the eye and small side fin, allowing again a margin of about $\frac{1}{8}$ inch for correction at a later stage.

Now, very carefully cutting in towards the edge of the eye and fin, sink a channel down to a depth of about $\frac{1}{8}$ inch. Great care must be taken in this operation to prevent the gouge from slipping and removing portions of the eye or fin.

When this is done the rest of the wood on the body can be carefully reduced with the broader, spade-shaped tool. Try to make the cuts evenly and in a fairly uniform direction so far as the grain will allow, as this will make good practice in the use of the tool.

As yet, there has been no attempt to make the curved section of the body of the fish: everything is rather cut at right angles. This carving of the form will come soon. With practice it may be achieved at the earlier stage, but for the purpose of this instruction it is as well to tackle the work in this rather angular fashion, and it helps us to check that the work is evenly balanced as we proceed.

With a spade-shaped, flatter gouge (figure 25) the fins and tail may be thinned down and evened out a stage further.

If we examine a fish from the top or plan view, we notice that the body is tapered gradually towards the tail end and also, more bluntly, at the head end, giving it a streamlined shape so that it may slide through the water more easily. So at this stage gradually taper the body down at the tail and head, ensuring all the time that the work is evenly balanced on both sides.

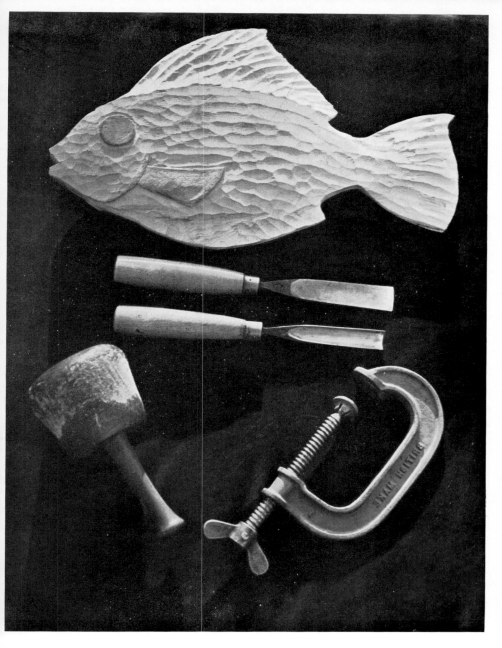

23. *The outlines of the eye and small fin have been cut round and the rest of the wood removed from the body. The commencement of the tapering of the body is evident: the outline has been carried a stage further*

CARVING A FISH . 4

We are now ready to commence the actual form of the body of the fish, that is to carve the body into the narrow oval shape, or section. On each side divide the body into approximately equal parts horizontally with a pencil or charcoal line from the nose to the tail. This serves as a rough guide line from which to commence the gouge strokes. Using the flattish spade tool, begin to remove wood carefully from this line towards the outline of the body, arranging the cuts to become deeper at the edge. Repeat these strokes along all edges and sides.

Care must be taken to ensure that the gouge does not slip and cut into the fins or tail, and also that none of the protruding shape of the eye or small fins is chipped or removed.

Try to keep the cutting at a uniform depth, because these cuts are forming practically the finished surface level of the body. The mallet may be laid aside, too, at this stage, and small uniform cuts made over the surface with a $\frac{1}{4}$- or $\frac{3}{8}$-inch flat sweep gouge.

Examine the work from time to time in a good side or top light, and notice if the true oval form of the fish's body is emerging from the wood without undue hollows or bumps. Work carefully with the small flattish gouge, making small cuts all over the surface in as uniform and regular manner as you can manage. Be careful not to cut the wood away at an angle between the body and fin and tail, rather let the shape sweep gradually one into the other.

When you are satisfied that the body is evenly carved, give the same treatment to the fins and tail, not worrying about the decorative lines in them, but rather preparing a ground into which these can be carved. See that the fins and tail, taper off to a fairly thinnish edge, thus preventing a too clumsy and heavy appearance.

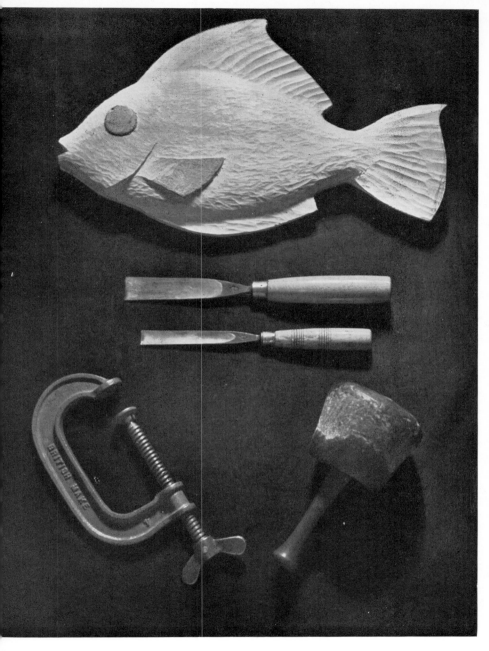

24. *The smooth oval section of the body is carved, the fins and tail thinned down still more,
and the cutting lines of the gouge have suggested the rhythmic lines on these parts. The
pieces forming the eye and small fin have not as yet been touched*

At this stage we must decide upon the surface finish of our carving.

In the present instance, I have treated the two sides of the fish differently; that in figure 25 being left with the marks of the tool, and careful cutting of the decorative fluting on the fins and tail, and with the eye carved decoratively; the other side (figure 26) has been carved to an even surface and then all tool marks have been removed with rifflers and finally sand-paper to give a smooth even finish; details have been ignored, the larger, interesting forms studied and emphasised.

Examine the two finishes carefully. The first I would call the carver's approach, that is the craftsman is interested in the surface and treatment which the use and choice of his tools dictate, the decorative value being important.

The second treatment I would call the sculptor's approach, satisfaction being derived from the simplicity of the big shapes, their subtleties, relation to each other, and the whole being treated more as a shape, rather than as a decorative rendering of a fish.

Notice in the carver's treatment the lines of the flutings on the fins and tail; they are not parallel with each other but radiate or spring from one point, and gradually spread rather fanwise towards the edges; the lines are fairly evenly spaced. It is important to realise this rhythm in nature; the lines on the horns of goats; the growth of leaves on a branch: the veining of leaves; the grouping and massing of the feathers in a bird's wing; all have this radiation and graduation.

Pencil-in these lines on the parts to be carved, and with a small curved gouge carefully remove a channel between each of the pencil lines. Now this channel may be broadened almost up to the pencil lines. Great care must be exercised in this work; it may be necessary to change the direction of the cuts when the grain is considered. Fluting is a very good exercise in the handling of the gouges and should be accomplished without the use of the mallet.

The carving of the eye is self-explanatory, I think.

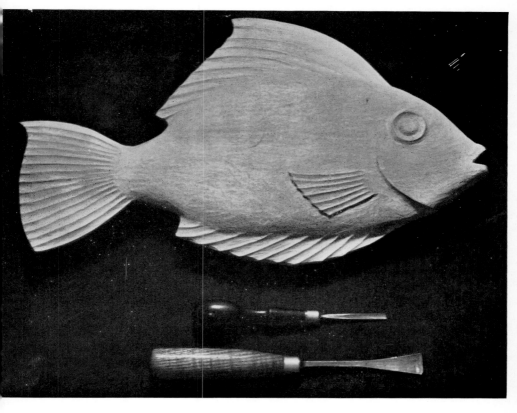

25.   *The carver's approach, with the tool marks left to enhance the decorative value*

CARVING A FISH . 6

In sculptural treatment notice how certain sharpnesses and edges are preserved. The smoothing-off of the shape must be done with a great deal of discretion, and a good side or top light to study and examine the work is very important to reveal any unnecessary undulations which would spoil the big main shapes.

Notice how even the eye has been simplified and treated as a slightly raised spherical disc. A certain amount of movement has been given to the tail and upper fin; notice finally how the grain of the wood is revealed in this smooth treatment.

Keep the wood as clean as possible.

26.   *The sculptor's approach, with the interest expressed entirely in the shapes*

27. OWEN BROUGHTON.
Porpoise. Tasmanian blackwood,
height 13 inches (from *Sculpture, Theme and Variations* by
E. H. Ramsden, courtesy Lund
Humphries)

MOVEMENT

The description of the carving of our fish has been somewhat of a stage-by-stage nature, leaving little to the imagination, and rather a striving after the ability to produce a carving in wood. I have purposely kept the subject quite straight and static in its position, as I feel the difficulties in carving even this must be very great to a beginner, but the exercise to produce something which has both sides alike will have been of great help.

28. P. EDWARD NORMAN. Group of swimming fish forming part of a series of carvings for R.M.S. Queen Elizabeth. Mahogany, height 30 inches. An attempt has been made to give a downward movement

It might occur to the beginner that it would be rather fun to introduce movement and life into our subject, the wriggly, rhythmic movement of the fish as it dives and turns and swims through the water.

Make another quick clay sketch of the fish as you did at first. Now give its body a slight bend, and the tail a twist, and also perhaps introduce a slight undulation in the back fin. You will notice immediately how these little movements have given a feeling of life to the sketch, the fish is swimming and moving in its natural element. Draw a centre line with a pointed piece of wood, or a wire, all round the centre line of the edges of the fish, and notice how our precious straight guide line has been bent and moved, and notice also that a thicker piece of wood would be needed to accommodate these curves and movements in our subject.

If you have time and a piece of material of the necessary size, try another carving of the fish, and this time try to get this movement into it; notice how one side will curve in while the opposite side curves out. Sketch-in the movement of the centre line when you have completed the outline, then try to carve your subject with this movement.

The problems will be somewhat greater than in the first one, but with patience and observation of the clay sketch I think you will be able to manage.

DESIGN AND SIMPLIFICATION

Have you noticed that in things which are moving—living creatures, aircraft, fast boats, etc.—the superficial details are very subsidiary to the line and rhythm of the movement? If we try to portray speed in a sketch, the lines of the movement are the main essentials put down on paper. So it is I think in carving the beauty of movement of a fish in water, a bird in flight, a deer leaping: we are not aware of the scales of the fish, or

29. D. CUMMINGS. *Animal Form.* Notice the sharpness here and there and how they help to prevent any feeling of flabbiness

the feathers of the bird or the texture of the hide of the deer. Indeed, if we attempt to indicate these faithfully, they immediately arrest our impression of the movement, and rather tend to turn the subject into a realistic photographic model. This love of detail, and the technical ability to achieve it, was very evident in work of the last century but the work so often lacked vitality of movement that the impression was lost.

So it is with our humble carvings. A swimming fish carved with little detail in a piece of wood such as lignum vitae or rosewood, which will take a high polish when finished, will give us more satisfaction as a work of art than a laboriously carved detailed study of the fish as it might appear in a glass case in a museum.

This problem of simplification is a very difficult one to understand, and can only really be appreciated by doing more and more work oneself, studying work both historical and contemporary, and comparing notes on the interpretations that various sculptors have given.

Often the actual texture of the grain of the wood used will be all that is necessary to suggest the scales or fur or hair of a subject, and this is enhanced by a smooth polished finish of its surface. So often we hear that abrasives (sand-paper, etc.) should never be used in carving. This is a rather old-fashioned idea, from a time when the carver and the technique he used was of paramount importance. But if we look at carvings by the Egyptians or Greeks, or medieval work, how often we find the surface has been scraped and polished, all marks of the tool erased. The effect of the finished work, its meaning, is all important, not how it was achieved. If a subject is going to be improved by a smooth, sleek finish, then by all means let us achieve this smoothness; this does not necessarily mean smoothing off every part of the crispness of the carving. This smooth finish will call for a much more careful searching for the main planes of the work, an emphasis here and there on the edge and change of direction, a sharpness which will give contrast to the flowing smoothness of the form. Removal of edges of planes and changes of direction of the main forms will only result in a flabby, soapy quality, lacking any character, strength or meaning. It is a good idea sometimes to make a carving leaving the whole of the work in this cubist form; it does help one to realise more and more the necessity of an accurate search for the planes in form.

30. P. EDWARD NORMAN. *Walking Leopard.* Scotch fir, length 27 inches

TYPES OF CARVING

There are two main types of sculpture or carving:
1. Sculpture in the round, and 2. Sculpture in relief.

Sculpture in the round. In this we have a piece of work which is free standing; it fills a space, and generally is visible from all sides. This calls for a great deal of design so far as the rhythm of line, balance of mass and space, and the full use of light and shade is concerned. It is of great importance at all times, both during its conception and actual execution to make sure that these qualities are present, and during the early stages in particular a clay sketch or model is invaluable and practically indispensable. Its great value is that it may be easily altered to improve an idea, or an alternative idea may be tried out, before the problem is tackled in wood for, once the wood is removed with the gouge, it is impossible to replace it.

Have the piece of wood you intend to use for a carving standing by while the clay sketch is being made, as the dimensions and form of the wood can be used to restrict the clay model, thus making one realise at all times the limitations that the wood imposes on the design of the work.

The value of the clay sketch again is in the fact that it helps one to realise which will be the best direction of the grain for the finished work, so that thin and dangerous pieces are not in the short direction of the grain.

When the clay sketch has been made and allowed to become leather hard, it is a good idea to place a piece of thin material such as butter muslin, or thin linen, over it and tie it fairly tight at the bottom or in some fashion so that the intricacies of the clay sketch are hidden and merely a basic shape is evident. This is useful both for assessing the approximate proportions of the block of wood and the preliminary bosting out of the main shape with the larger gouges. It prevents any unnecessary deep portions or undercuts being made at too early a stage; it allows us to fix on the high points, which we can chalk or mark on the wood, and tends to simplify the subject down to its main planes.

Remember at all times however that the clay sketch is only a suggestion and no attempt should be made to copy it exactly, as that will only tend to make the wood carving dull and slavish, and will not allow the true character of the material to assert itself, which after all is of primary importance.

31. P. EDWARD NORMAN. Abstract. Carved from a block of plaster this is a preliminary to work out some problems before the work is tackled in wood. Notice the use of convex and concave shapes, the contrast of masses and the use of sharp and rounded forms

As you do more and more carving the use of the clay sketch may be dispensed with altogether, because you will have learned to visualise your finished work while viewing the uncut piece of wood which you intend to use. When this stage is reached and you are able to carve direct, the finished result will be lively, inventive and stimulating.

Work in the round depends a great deal for its success on its interesting and well-composed silhouette form, this form being maintained as much as possible from every angle. A sense of instability should be avoided, as nothing is more disconcerting than a piece of work which looks as though it will topple over or move away at any movement.

Sculpture in relief. In this the subject matter is not represented in its full three dimensions, but rather more as a picture in which the objects stand out a little from the background. The pattern of the design has to have considerable importance, so that the result as a whole is self-contained. There must be variety in the massing and spacing, and the background at all times must have the least importance.

The subject matter itself should be bold and direct, the space well and completely filled. It is surprising how thin and weak a design becomes in which the spaces have been allowed to have larger areas than need be. The whole design should, in my opinion, have a certain amount of flat quality. By this I mean that the carving should not appear as a space in a wall, in which distance and perspective have been allowed to take their full part. One should remember at all times that the carving is a piece of design and should be treated as such. Colour and atmosphere, sunshine and rain, are practically impossible to obtain, and our effect at all times depends on subtle form.

I do not feel that the grain or figure of the wood is of such importance in this type of work. Relief carving as a whole is rather akin to drawing with the wood, and the actual technique of the toolmarks used, as opposed to the completely smoothed quality of the work in the round, is important.

Relief carving again varies from low, or bas-relief, up to the full relief in which subjects are worked up to practically three-quarters of their full third dimension.

The position of light and shade is extremely important in relief carving and should be considered at an early stage of its execution, the work being carried out in lighting similar to that in which it will be when completed and *in situ*. This will enable full value to be placed on the subtle planes and edges in the work, which would otherwise probably be lost.

Details such as hair, eyes, folds, etc., must all be considered in their correct tonal relation to the rest of the work, otherwise they will be too strong in their contrasting light and shadow effects.

Another use of the relief panel is in pierced relief, that is where the background is actually cut away or pierced through, so that the background against which the work is eventually placed is of importance in the design.

32. IVAN MESTROVIC. *Deposition*, 38 x 64 inches. Reproduced by courtesy of the Trustees of the Tate Gallery, London. This beautiful relief carving with its strong emotional appeal emphasizes the composition and pattern effect, the masterly filling of the space, all achieved within the minimum of depth

The placing and size of the piercing will need careful consideration, and it is a good scheme, when originally designing the panel on paper, to silhouette in solid black the subject matter leaving the paper for the piercings. This will also enable you to see that the various pieces are tied together correctly.

Foreshortening should be avoided as much as possible, and the design should be a direct statement. I think one can do no better than study some of the exquisite medieval ivory carvings in relief, for their emphasis on important points, directness of statement, their surface treatments and enrichments, and the wonderful completeness of the finished work: also heraldic carvings and devices, which again have this directness, with little or no attempt at foreshortening or perspective qualities.

Great as the relief carvings of Grinling Gibbons are, one is even more amazed and astonished at the detail, distance and accuracy in such a work as his *The Stoning of St. Stephen* now at the Victoria and Albert Museum, London. The feeling of pattern or flatness and the material used is necessarily of secondary importance, and one is left with an actual scene, a three-dimensional picture.

33. P. LUCK. *St. George and the Dragon*, height 24 inches. A spirited relief carving: the composition and pattern effect is very satisfactory and the interest caused by the various textures is successful. Perhaps one or two passages are inclined to be a little thin and papery and little accidents, such as the hand holding the spear, might have been avoided

49

34. P. EDWARD NORMAN. Pierced relief
panel, ebony, height 11 inches. An attempt has
been made to emulate the negro quality of
carving. Notice the use of the cut-away spaces
to help the subject matter to be more clearly
indicated

35. DOUGLAS WAIN-HOBSON.   *Angel*,
birchwood, height 42 inches (collection of Sir
Alan Barlow).   This decorative figure relies for
effect on its precision of carving in the hair and
the folds and is left with its direct tool cuts

SURFACE TREATMENT

The finished surface treatment of the work is largely a matter of individual taste, type of wood and subject matter. A very careful gouge-cut finish is attractive, and the direction of the cuts may be used to emphasise a form. It is also valuable in hair or fur renderings, and serves a very useful means of obtaining texture in both relief and in the round.

If the wood is one such as lignum vitae or rosewood, which will take a high, natural polish, then this quality may be used to advantage, but the surface should be flawless, as any irregularity or unnecessary undulation of the surface is exaggerated by the high polish and the resulting lights and reflected lights.

A combination of smooth finish and chip finish may sometimes be used with good results.

Great discretion should be used when reaching the finished surface stage. Above all else, the *form* should always be maintained, and not rubbed away and softened by the cruel use of sandpaper. The size of the work will to some extent influence the surface form.

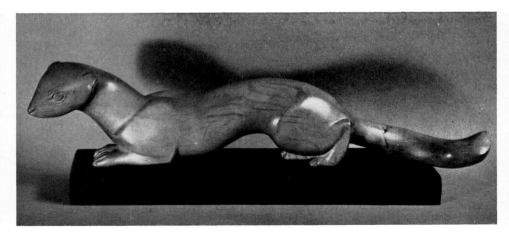

36. P. EDWARD NORMAN. *Marten*, boxwood, length 13 inches. This carving relies for effect on its smoothness and sleekness

INSPIRATION

Very often a problem which arises is what to carve in a piece of wood.

I feel that some of the best sources of inspiration come from such simple objects as sea shells and pebbles, which have been turned into interesting shapes by the sea's action; leaves, so varied and beautiful in their forms, bud forms, cactii, sea life, animal life, and lastly the human form itself.

All these objects will need to be studied, and their decorative value, rhythmic lines, balance of shapes, etc., noted: even their markings may suggest the use of a particular piece or type of wood which will help to convey their form. We should not attempt to copy one of them slavishly, but use it as a guide or an inspiration for the realisation of a carving. It may be necessary to exaggerate the thickness of a portion, or the curve of a line, and possibly the elimination of the undercutting in some parts,

37. Actual plant forms, direct inspiration for subjects, from Karl Blossfeldt's *Art Forms in Nature* (courtesy A. Zwemmer Ltd.)
right. Limewood carving based on plant form, height 2 feet

38. R. E. GOWER. *Shell*, length about 7 inches. The shell on the left was the inspiration for this carving. Notice how the form has been simplified a little and the surface finished to a high degree. Carved in laurel, it is a pleasure to see and feel

bearing in mind at all times that we are translating into our own particular medium, and letting its limitations naturally impose themselves. The medieval craftsman made a great deal of use of these various natural forms in his stone and wood carvings, ceiling bosses, capitals, etc., and there is always evident in them, simplification, decorative value and realisation of the material's demands which in no way detract from a delightful lively quality.

The study of historical works is invaluable to the artist and craftsman and whenever possible one should look at work done by great craftsmen of the past, and note how particular passages such as detail of hair, hands, feet, drapery, foliage, texture of fur or scales of sea monsters, etc., have been tackled and solved. Your sketchbook should always be handy, for these points jotted down in it will prove extremely useful at some time or another in your own work. I would stress this for I have sometimes found young students reluctant to make use of sketches or references for their work. They will grope about on their own trying to invent shapes and forms which have never existed and which are invariably so much uglier than the ones which Nature herself has provided.

54

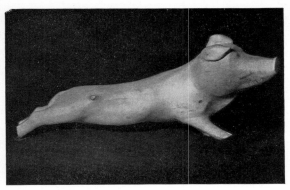

39. ARNOLD MACHIN, ARA, *Pig*, London plane (collection of Tom Wedgwood Esq)

40. *right:* P. EDWARD NORMAN. *The Dancer*, lignum vitae, height 7 inches. Rhythm and movement through a simplified figure

41. Plan from Karl Blossfeldt's *Art Forms in Nature* (A. Zwemmer)

42. Growing plant form, teak, height 16 inches. The approach is rather similar to that of *The Dancer*

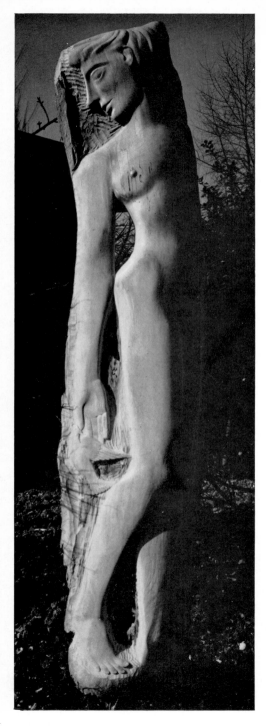

43.

FRANTA BELSKY, F.R.B.S., A.R.C.A.,
Spring. Beech 6 feet high. The beech
was found on the ground in Burnham
Beeches. It is a segment, the bark
was still outside the sapwood but the
heart rotted away leaving about 2 inches
of sound timber. The sculptor made
use of the two undulations, one for the
arm, and the other for the body and
has left the original outline of the
log untouched.

The gouge was used in the early
stages followed by a spoke shave, a
fine chisel and plenty of sandpaper
down to oo. The work was finally
polished with beeswax.

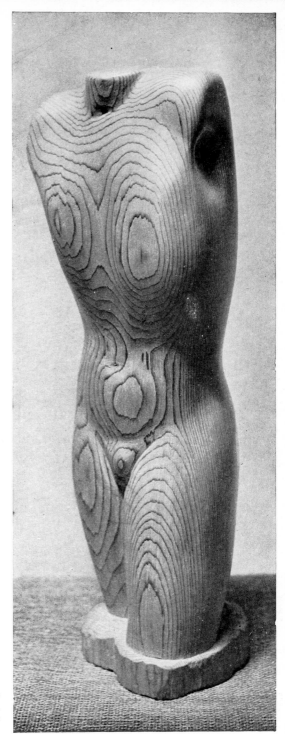

44. ELFORD COX, *Torso*, cedar
(collection of Douglas Duncan Esq).
Notice the delightful effect of the
grain on this form

SCULPTURAL QUALITY

One should attempt at all times to maintain a sculptural quality in one's work. It is always best to err a little on the thicker or more massive side, particularly in parts of the figure like the neck or the ankles, legs and arms. It is surprising how weak a carving of a figure will appear if strict adherence to the true proportions in these parts is enforced; also in the edges of drapery or clothing: if carved faithfully they will appear thin, edgy and papery, particularly if undercutting is carried out to any great extent. When carving or scheming a piece of work remember all the time that it is going to be a translation into another material, wood, which will impose limitations and restrictions but which, happily, will enhance the value of the work if used to the right purpose.

It is surprising how often to the layman a work of art is indicated by intricate and trivial details achieved possibly through very clever technique, while the greater qualities of simplicity and refinement are overlooked. Contrast the massive heads and figures of some of the great Egyptian carvings, necessarily simplified by the great technical difficulties imposed by the materials, with the fussy and detailed carvings of the rococo or French Empire periods.

Few people realise the beauty of woods themselves: the beautiful grain and figuring, varying so much with a change of light, and an interesting shape formed by the natural growth of a trunk or branch of a tree, more often than not needs but a small amount of work on the part of the sculptor to realise an idea or theme which nature has already provided.

45. *opposite:* P. LUCK. *Bear*, length about 16 inches. All the forms and the wood chosen help to show the massive, heavy quality of the bear. Note the little sharpnesses and changes of plane which prevent the work becoming flabby and ballooning

46. J. ROWE. *Animal Form*, birch, length 7 inches. This decorative animal has been kept quite bold in form and treatment, the student having in mind its use as a door-knocker

59

ABSTRACT

It gives me a great sense of satisfaction to carve a piece of wood, paying particular attention to the feel of the shape and the surface obtained. Ignoring subject matter and creating a simple yet dignified shape, a thing we call abstract, needs artistic and sensitive expression.

Simple natural forms, an egg, a pebble, a bud, can lend themselves well as basic shapes. Even to take these forms and carve them, many times

47. A. S. GARBUTT. *Abstract*, oak, length about 11 inches

larger, in an interesting wood such as walnut, elm, chestnut or lignum vitae, or even a piece of ebony, with very little departure from the form of the natural object, and paying particular attention to the finished surface, will result in a very stimulating piece of work.

The egg or pebble shape can then be experimented with, concave surfaces cut in, holes bored through and carved into interesting voids, bearing a relationship to the complete shape. This will call for a great deal of artistic endeavour and it is worth while to experiment in this way, bearing in mind at all times that you are not attempting to represent, but to form an interesting shape, pleasant and exciting to the eye and the touch.

60

48. BARBARA HEPWORTH. *Pelagos*, wood with blue interior and strings, height 16 inches (collection of Duncan Macdonald Esq.)

Study some of the beautiful abstract carvings by contemporary sculptors: notice how the choice of wood, direction of grain, and beautiful surface and finish, all combine to help the finished piece of work.

49. BARBARA HEPWORTH. *The   Wave*, wood with colour and string, length 18 inches (collection Ashley Havinden Esq)

JOINING WOOD

It is not always possible to obtain wood of a sufficient size for a particular piece of work. In this case, the wood may be joined or laminated. Care should be taken to see that the grain is matching as closely as possible and running in the same direction, and unless one has done joining it is advisable to take the wood to a local carpenter, who will no doubt shoot the sides and glue and clamp up for you. A good joint in wood requires a great deal of skill, and nothing is more annoying than a piece of work ruined by the joints opening or coming apart.

50. The back of a violin carved from two pieces of sycamore or maple matched and chosen for their lovely figure. Great accuracy is needed in the modelling and thinning of the wood to obtain the correct tone

51. J. PEAT. *Bird*, cedar, length 17 inches. The two pieces used in this subject were joined down the centre line to allow the marked grain to balance along the back

Sometimes the joining of the grain may be used to enhance the decorative value of the work.

Good glues, such as Croid or Scotch, must always be used, and this applies also to the replacement of small pieces which may be chipped off or damaged, either while carving or when the work is completed. If you are going to do these small repairs yourself, first see that the portion fits correctly. Get the glue hot and with hot water wet both places to be joined: this will swell the grain slightly and allow the glue to penetrate.

Apply the glue to the faces with a small brush, bring them immediately into contact, and clamp up or bind securely, wiping off the surplus glue with a rag or brush dipped in the hot water. When the job is thoroughly dry (leave it for at least twelve hours) the clamp or binding may be removed and the surfaces carefully cleaned down to conceal the joint.

Some of the new resin glues may be used, but these set extremely hard and may be injurious to the carving tools if more carving has to be done;

52. A. HALL. *Torso*

they are, however, extremely strong and easy to handle.

Cracks will often appear in the wood as it is being carved. Do not worry about these, as more often than not they will close up again. If not they should be filled with softened beeswax. This will conceal the crack and at the same time allow the wood to move or close up again. Do not attempt to put wedges of wood into the crack, as this may only lead to further cracking as the wood moves.

WAXING AND POLISHING

Wood which has been freshly carved has a cleanliness about it which unfortunately can soon be lost, particularly if the wood is of a light colour; moisture and dirt from the hands will soon impair its pristine quality.

This may be prevented by polishing the work with a wax polish rubbed really well into the surface. The wax may be prepared by cutting up pieces of beeswax, placing them in a metal tin and covering with turpentine. Gently heat this by putting the metal tin into a shallow saucepan of hot water, so that the turpentine does not catch alight, and seeing that the beeswax is thoroughly melted. This may be left to cool and then applied to the surface of the carving very thinly with a piece of thin cloth. With another clean rag the surface should be rubbed vigorously all over, and a smooth even polish will result. Not only does this protect the surface of the wood from dirt and the effect of dampness, but it also enhances its grain.

French polishing, staining or cellulosing should never be applied to wood sculpture, as the resultant polish is hard and rather commercial in appearance.

A very fine surface may be achieved on the carving by burnishing it with another piece of hard wood. This will give a perfectly natural polish to the surface and is extremely attractive.

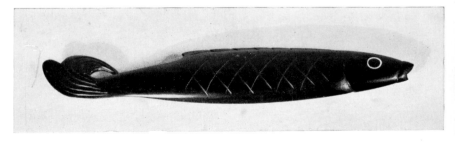

53. J. PEAT. *Paper knife*, African ironwood with metal inlaid eye, length about 7 inches

DESIGNING THE BASE

The selection of a suitable base for a carving is not always such a simple matter as may at first appear. Its proportion, thickness and width in relation to the carving is of extreme importance. One should feel that the base is part of the whole design, and not merely a slab.

A tall carving may be enhanced by a tall base, its sides tapering in perhaps a little to meet and carry on the eye through the form. A carving with many curves and twists in its design may be emphasised by a simple and somewhat severe block, and a carving which has severity as its keynote may need just a touch of enrichment in the form of the base on which it stands. The base at all times should be subsidiary to the carving; one should be conscious of it, but it should not shout. Perhaps a contrasting colour wood and change of material will be the note that is required to 'complete' the piece of sculpture.

Try standing your work on a box, or a book, or even make a simple base in clay; experiment in its proportion and form, see the work on its base in a mirror to get a fresh eye and viewpoint on the work.

The question of fixing the work to its base (when this is necessary or desirable) presents little problem. Draw with a pencil line on the top of the base round the base of the carving, having stood it in its correct and most obvious position. Remove the carving and mark with a pencil two spots far enough from the outline to prevent the carving from splitting when screws are inserted; drill two holes vertically through to the bottom of the base.

Turn the base over, and from the bottom drill two countersunk holes large enough and deep enough to allow some stout wood screws to pass up through. Screws sufficiently long for part to enter the underside of the carving must be used.

Remove the screws, place the base and carving back into position, and mark through the holes two corresponding points in the carving. These points may then be drilled sufficiently to allow the screws to take a hold. It is as well to use brass screws to prevent any rusting discolouring the wood, and to dip them in a little grease before they are screwed home.

CONCLUSION

54. P. EDWARD NORMAN. *Faun,* mahogany, height 30 inches. One of a series for R.M.S. Queen Elizabeth

The art of the sculptor is vast. Years of experience, practical knowledge and artistic creative endeavour; a natural feel for the wood, its growth, colour, texture, its weaknesses and its strength; the use of the tools and their right selection for a particular passage are things which become a part of the sculptor.

It would be an impossible task to instill all of these into anyone in such a short space as this book permits, but if it has opened the way and made suggestions, both from a practical and an aesthetic point of view, then it will have served its purpose. It will have done more; it will have opened up the possibilities, the stimulating and exciting urge to create, through your eye and hand, and the medium of wood, objects of interest and value in this age of mechanical mass production.

You will have become a wood sculptor.

68

55. High officer of state in full court dress, Egyptian 18th dynasty (*c.* 1400 B.C.) height 11 inches. British Museum, Salt collection

56. *Ointment spoons* with the handles designed as a figure of a young girl with a pole
in the marshes (*above*), and as a woman with
elaborate head-dress. 1250 B.C. (*right*). Lengths
6½ and 9¼ inches. British Museum

The extremely high standard achieved in ancient Egyptian carving is seen in the
examples in figures 55 & 56. Note the direct decorative quality of the folds and hair
and the somewhat static pose of the figure carved in relation to the dimensions of
the wood. The spoons are treated decoratively and are perfect statements in relief

57. *Country hare*, 1250 B.C. length
14 inches, British Museum. A
beautiful simplified animal form,
which one feels could only be
carved in wood: the masses are
well balanced and raised. Study
and compare it with some contemporary work, note the similarity
in the simplicity and bigness of
approach

58.   *Christ on the cross* (detail)
from Spydeberg, Norway, *c.* 1260.
Oslo University Museum of Antiquities. This head of Christ, sensi-
tively carved, broad in treatment,
and with so much feeling is very
typical of the wood sculptor's art
in the thirteenth century. The
panels show the richness and story-
telling interest of early work

59. End panels of a boxwood casket depicting scenes from the life of Christ. Southern French or Spanish, 12th century. Victoria and Albert Museum, Crown copyright

60. *Coffer*. Byzantine, 12th century. Victoria and Albert Museum, Crown copyright

61. Detail of doorway from Hyle-
stad, Setesdal, showing scenes
from the tale of Sigurd in Nor-
wegian mythology, late 12th century, Oslo University Museum of
Antiquities. All these carvings in
relief are rich in pattern and form.
Note the treatment of the tree and
the birds, and the way in which
practically every part of each piece
is designed decoratively. There is
little attempt at foreshortening

62. *Pillar*. South Italian, 12th-13th century.
Victoria and Albert Museum, Crown copyright

63. *Boxwood staff*. French, 13th century,
height 4 feet. Victoria and Albert Museum,
Crown copyright

64. *Carved head.* Spanish or French 12th century, courtesy M. R. Taylor Esq. (photo: F. Fortt)

65. *Virgin and Child*. English, late 12th century, oak, height 18½
inches. Victoria and Albert Museum, Crown copyright.   This group
although unfortunately so mutilated, has the same bigness and true
wood-like quality as the later Flemish group in figure 76

66. *St. Peter*. 13th-15th century, height 19L inches. Victoria and Albert Museum. Crown copyright. Compare this carving with that in figure 68. It is a little more static but the forms are well designed and carved, large and simplified, and the complete work forms a very fine piece of sculpture

67. *Head of Christ*. From South Cerney, Glos. Courtesy Courtauld Institute of Art

68. *St. John the Evangelist*. Spanish 14th century, walnut, height 14 inches. Victoria
and Albert Museum, Crown copyright. Although marked by the passage of time this
head is a superb piece of sculpture. The pose, the depth of feeling and the conception
of the complete composition is wholly satisfactory

69. *Coffer-front* (detail), depicting St. George and the Dragon. English, late 14th century, oak, 57 x 25¼ inches. Victoria and Albert Museum, Crown copyright. Here is the art of relief carving at its best; the complete feeling of design and pattern in the panel as a whole. The quaint exaggeration of relative proportions, giving a flat perspective, should be noted. Individually the level in the town, the treatment of the walls, roofs and windows, the decoration of the trees, the undulation of the foreground and the little animals hiding and peeping from their burrows: all serve their purpose

70. *Misericord* from St. Nicholas Chapel, King's Lynn. English, *c.* 1415, height 12 inches. Victoria and Albert Museum, Crown copyright

71. *Figure of a King.* Flemish, late 15th century, height 23½ inches. Victoria and Albert Museum, Crown copyright

72. VEIT STOSS. Head from Church of Our Lady, Cracow, late 15th century. Courtesy Courtauld Institute of Art, photo: S. Kolowca

73. *The Angels appearing to the shepherds announcing the birth of Christ.* Exeter Cathedral, oak, height about 30 inches. This group again shows how the complete subject has been designed within the limitations of the wood. It tells its story directly and simply. Note the treatment of the flocks of sheep in the foreground

74. *Head of Christ*. From Lavandien, now in the Louvre. Courtesy Dr. G. Zarnecki

75. Probably from a Visitation group, from Terrington St. John Church, Norfolk. English, 15th century. Victoria and Albert Museum, Crown copyright. A lovely little figure sadly mutilated. Note the drapery and compare it with the drapery of *The Angel* by Douglas Wain-Hobson in figure 35

76. *Virgin and Child*. Flemish, 16th century, oak. Victoria and Albert Museum, Crown copyright. A strong sculptural group: the subject has been conceived and carved as a whole, the composition leading the eye towards the focal point, the Holy Child. There are no small, fussy pieces sticking out from the main shape; the drapery is bold and 'right'

77. A richly carved boxwood spoon. German, 1676. Victoria and Albert Museum, Crown copyright

78. *Charles II.* English, 17th century, height 19 inches, width 11 inches. Victoria and Albert Museum. Crown copyright. A masterly portrait bust and an example of extremely fine technique. But one feels that the medium has not been considered sufficiently: the work could have been as successfully accomplished in another medium, terracotta, bronze etc.

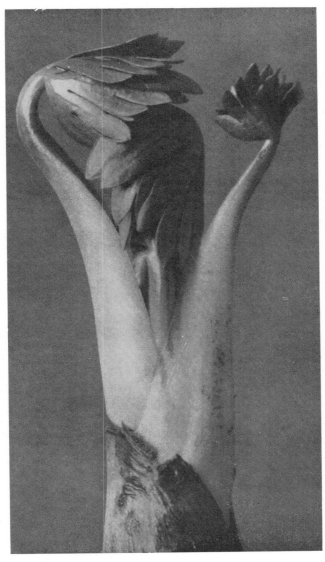

79. *Plant form.* From Prof. Karl Blossfeldt's *Art Forms in Nature,* courtesy A. Zwemmer Ltd. A direct idea for a piece of wood sculpture—a figure with arms raised

The carvings of the native always have directness and a complete understanding of the material. Note the very balanced, static quality of these pieces and the lovely touches of surface decoration

80. *left:* Ancestor figure from the Baluba tribe, eastern Congo, probably latter half of the 19th century. British Museum
81. *below:* Bapendi cup, western Congo, probably less than a year old when collected in 1907. British Museum

82. Portrait statue of Shamba Bolongongo, from Kasai Province, Congo, probably carved about 1800. British Museum

83. Chief's stool from the Baluba tribe, eastern Congo, probably late 19th century. British Museum

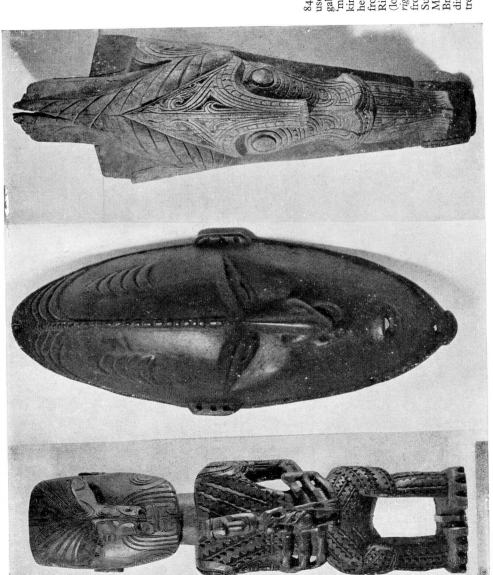

84-86. *left*: Maori image used as a house post or gable ornament with 'moko' decorations of the kind used on human heads; *centre*: mask from the Lower Sepik River, New Guinea (loaned by Ralph Linton); *right*: carved beam end from a Batak house, Sumatra (loaned by Colin McPhee). Courtesy of the Brooklyn Museum. Three direct carvings with extremely rich surface treatment

90

68

88

87. *above*: Dancing mask of the Baule tribe, Ivory Coast, col-
oured wood, with red, white, ochre and black. This and the
amusing 'giraffe' spoons (figures 88-90) show the appeal of the
animal form

91. Modern Ashanti umbrella top, illustrating the proverb 'the snake crawls in the grass, but God has given him the hornbill'. Height 19½ inches. British Museum. A piece of modern carving interesting from the point of view of its silhouette and balanced shapes

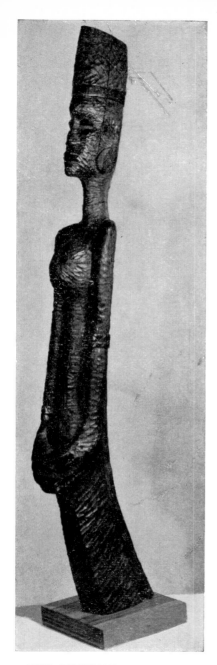

92. BEN ENWONWU. *Fulani*, ebony.
Galerie Apollinaire. The direct influence of
the shape of the material before carving.
Very little wood has had to be removed
to release the idea.   Note the direct tool
marks on the surface

93. MORLEY TROMAN. *Nude*,
(Galerie Drouant-David, Paris)

94. EDWARD CARTE
PRESTON, *Figure*, ye

95. P. EDWARD NORMAN. *Marine*, lime, length 11 inches. Rhythm and movement of the sea, shapes of shells, erosion of rocks and pebbles, all have influenced this piece

96. ROBERT ADAMS. *Figure*, laburnum
height 13½ inches

Two contrasting abstract
carvings, one relying
mainly on curves the
other on rather straight
lines. The quality of the
material used in each is
noteworthy

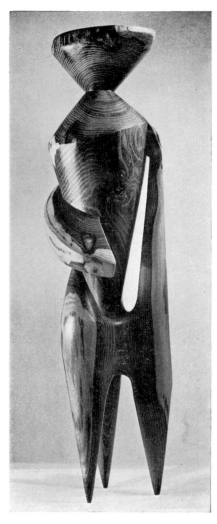

97. GERALD LEWERS. Totemhead,
bogwood

98. GIBBON GRINLING. *Family group*, cedar

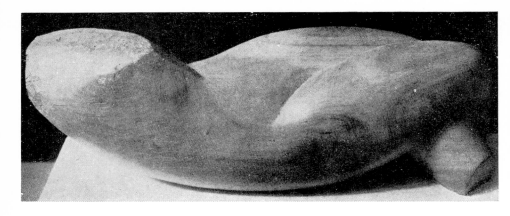

99. ORONZIO MALDARELLI. *Torso*, (Boyer Galleries, New York)

100. Gibbons Grinling. *Judy*, mahogany

101. K. C. FORD. *Allegory of the Church*, holly wood, height 4 feet

102. DOUGLAS WAIN-HOBSON. *Head of a Saint*, elm, life size. A fine example of forceful direct carving, influenced by the work of the Gothic craftsmen

103. GENNI MUCCHI. *Il torturato*

104. *bottom left: Benedictine monk*, 18th century, limewood, polychromed

105. *bottom right:* DOMINIC BIL-INSKI. *St. George*, limewood. The similarity to medieval work in treatment and expression is apparent in these Polish peasant carvings. Note how the St. George juts well into the block

106. JOHN BUNTING. Corbels for Old Palace, Oxford. English oak.
Compare these boldly carved corbels with the relief panels in figure 59;
telling the story of Adam and Eve, they have a rich quality of light and
shade and read well from a distance

107. EDNA MANLEY. *Horse of the Morning*, life size (courtesy of Michael Manley). A vigorous and exciting piece of sculpture, full of life and movement, with rich surface treatment and regard for the basic shape of the wood used

108. EWALD MATARE. *Horse*, Hamburg Museum für Kunst und Gewerbe. A complete subject treated as a shape, not a copy, of a horse, the limitations and quality of the wood asserting itself